REALITY BASED DECISION MAKING FOR EFFECTIVE STRATEGY DEVELOPMENT

By Jennifer Hancock

Published by Jennifer Hancock

Copyright 2018 by Jennifer Hancock

Published 2018

CreateSpace Edition

ISBN-13: 978-1985176140

ISBN-10: 1985176149

This book is also available in electronic and audiobook format at most online retailers

Discover other titles by Jennifer Hancock at:
https://humanistlearning.com/jennifer-hancock/

Take the online course at:
https://humanistlearning.com/realitybaseddecisionmaking/

All rights reserved. No part of this book may be used or reproduced in any manner whatsoever without written permission, except in the case of brief quotations embodied in critical articles or reviews.

Table of Contents

CHAPTER 1: INTRODUCTION 5

CHAPTER 2: STRATEGIC PLANNING 101 9

CHAPTER 3: REALITY BASED DECISION MAKING 11

CHAPTER 4: SIX NECESSARY CRITICAL THINKING SKILLS 13

CHAPTER 5: PROXY PROBLEMS AND HOW TO AVOID THEM 17

CHAPTER 6: ROOT CAUSES & REAL PROBLEMS 19

CHAPTER 7: REAL SOLUTIONS TO REAL PROBLEMS ... 23

CHAPTER 8: EXAMPLES 27

CHAPTER 9: ABOUT THE AUTHOR: 33

CHAPTER 1: INTRODUCTION

Why this book:

This is the companion book to the online course: "Reality Based Decision Making for Effective Strategy Development." This book contains the transcripts of the online lessons compiled for easy home reference.

Strategies are important. They help us know what we are working on, why we are working on it and most importantly, how. The problem is, not all strategies are effective. In order to give yourself the best chance of success, it is important to take several steps to ensure that your strategy is reality based. This book will help you learn how to answer the three most important questions for any strategy. What is your real problem? What is really causing it and what will really work to solve it?

The online version of this course contains approximately 1 hour of video lessons and is facilitated. Participants can ask questions and receive feedback directly from the author, Jennifer Hancock.

To learn more or to register, please visit:
https://humanistlearning.com/realitybaseddecisionmaking/.

About the Author:

JENNIFER HANCOCK

I am the founder of Humanist Learning Systems. A big part of the humanist technique is to be strategic and reality based. I'm really good at strategy development. I am the person who created the strategy that got evolution written into Florida's Science Standards using just 3 people to get it done. This was mostly a set-it-in-motion and watch-it-play-out strategy. It took 3 people about 10 hours of time to do it. You might not like evolution in the standards, but the fact that I got it in there with so little effort, despite a well-organized opposition to it, is a testament to my abilities as a strategist.

DISCUSSION AND TOPICS COVERED

It doesn't matter what you want to do – a good strategy is important. Strategies help us know what we are working on, why we are working on it and most importantly, how. The problem is, not all strategies are effective. To give yourself the best chance of success, it is important to take several steps to ensure that your strategy is reality based. This book will help you learn how to answer the three most important questions for any strategy. What is your real problem? What is really causing it and what will really work to solve it?

The following are topics that I will discuss in this book:

- One simple technique to ensure you focus on your real problem and not a proxy problem

- Six critical thinking skills necessary to ensure your strategy is reality based

- How to evaluate your alternatives scientifically

Keep in mind that this book is meant to be a quick overview of reality based processes and techniques. There are concepts I will only introduce in this book but not get into detail on.

CHAPTER 2: STRATEGIC PLANNING 101

Let's start by defining what we are talking about. A strategy is not a goal, it is the way you plan to get to your goal.

If you are going to the supermarket there are probably many ways you can get there. You choose a route – and you go. The route is the strategy. Where you are going is the goal. But there is something else you need and that is a reason to go. No one just wants to go to the store. They go to the store for a reason. Don't ever develop a strategy without knowing the reason (the real reason) you are doing it. This is the most important part of any strategy and it's amazing how many people get this part wrong. The reason they get it wrong is because it seems obvious, but it isn't. They don't know why they are doing it, they just think they need to. People go to the supermarket all the time and forget what they went there to get, as I'm sure most of you have.

Let's assume you have a goal and you know why you want to achieve that goal. Now you want to create a strategy to get there. What you need now is a HEALTHY dose of reality! It doesn't matter if you know why you want to go to the supermarket, if you don't take into account reality, you probably won't make it there. It may seem silly when discussing going to the supermarket, but things happen, such as accidents that block the road which prevents you from getting to your destination.

If you think you can just go on your route straight there - in a straight line, A to B, you might find that there are houses in your way. Understanding what is in your way and what you have to get around to get to your destination is very important if you are actually going to get there.

CHAPTER 3: REALITY BASED DECISION MAKING

There are several aspects of problem solving that can benefit from taking a reality based approach. One question that we should ask is, what is your real problem? The main way people go wrong in strategy development is they try to solve the wrong problem, or worse, a problem that they don't actually have! I call these Proxy Problems. These are problems that stand in for your real problem, but aren't your real problem. Any time you spend time, energy, and money on proxy problems is time, energy, and money not spent on fixing your real problem.

Assuming that you know what your real problem is, the next place people go off course is they don't know what is really causing their problem. So they guess and guess wrong. Instead of fixing the underlying cause, they work on something that will have zero impact on their problem. This happens quite frequently. And again, if you are spending time, energy, and money on things that aren't going to impact the outcome of what you are working on, you are wasting time, energy, and money not fixing your real problem.

Finally, it isn't enough to know what your real problem is and what is really causing it, if you don't know what will really work to solve it. As I mentioned earlier, there are a lot of ways to go from A to B. Some routes will get you to your destination and some won't. You need to put effort into finding out which ones will really work and which ones really won't if you want to be successful.

CHAPTER 4: SIX NECESSARY CRITICAL THINKING SKILLS

To develop a realistic strategy, you have to find out what is real and what isn't. The best way to do that is to get in the habit of thinking critically.

There are six basic critical thinking skills that will help you learn what is real and what isn't. Here is a list of the necessary skills so you can start learning them.

First, **Analyze** your problem! Ask yourself why! Just being willing to question your assumptions will go a long way towards making sure your strategy is reality based. In fact, the question WHY – is the single most important question you can ask. What is your real problem and what is really causing it? That's two-thirds of a successful strategy right there. The remaining critical thinking skills will help you figure out what will really work to solve it. Get in the habit of asking yourself Why. I'm going to go into a lot more detail on exactly how "Why" works in the next chapter.

The next skill you need to learn is **Freethought**. Freethought is to think critically, yet freely. Like brainstorming, the easiest way to do this is by considering at least three options.

We all tend to think in terms of black or white. But, if you remember that sometimes things are grey, you will be way ahead of the game. Again, I'm going to discuss how exactly to apply this skill in another chapter, once we start talking about how to figure out the root cause of your problem.

Another skill is doing **Research**. Research will help you learn what is really causing your problem and what might really work to solve it. You need to research what doesn't work. If you think you have a solution that might work, look for evidence that it doesn't work. It is necessary to see both sides. Don't just look at the evidence that a vendor gives you and say – Wow, that looks like it works. Find out if it really does work before spending money on it!

This is why **Doubt and Skepticism** are such important critical thinking skills and why scientists and skeptics are always debunking things. A lot of people think of doubt and skepticism as negative thinking habits. They are actually really optimistic habits to have. People who doubt believe they can solve their problems, they just don't want to be duped into spending money, time, and resources on things that don't work.

Doubt and skepticism isn't enough though. In order to know what is real or not, you have to be able to evaluate the evidence. This requires a skill called **Scientific Literacy**. People who are scientifically literate know how to read and understand research papers. They don't have to take someone's word for it, they can actually evaluate the evidence presented and make a determination that the research is valid or not. This skill can be taught, and it's probably the most important skill to have in the modern age.

There are all sorts of claims about what is good and what is bad for you. Knowing what is BS and what is scientifically valid can save your life. People die all of the time from preventable diseases because they put their faith in "alternative" medicine, which is medicine that has no scientific evidence to support it.

The final critical thinking skill everyone should learn is how to identify **Logical Fallacies**.

Just because one thing is true, that doesn't mean what comes next is also true. Learning what fallacies are and how to identify them will help you determine whether what follows is valid and true, or not. What I recommend is that you go online and type in Fallacy and start reading the lists that people have posted online to begin understanding more.

CHAPTER 5: PROXY PROBLEMS AND HOW TO AVOID THEM

Let's focus on our first task, which is making sure that we are at least focused on solving our real problem and not a proxy problem.

Albert Einstein once said that if he had one hour to solve a problem, he would spend fifty minutes defining the problem. I can't stress enough how important it is that you make sure you are solving your real problem and not a proxy problem. The way to avoid proxy problems is to ask yourself "Why." Why do I want to solve this problem?

For example, let's say I'm a farmer and that my plants aren't growing due to a drought. I need to ask myself some questions. Why do I want it to rain? So I can get water on my field. Why do I want to get water on my field? So my plants will grow. Why do I want my plants to grow? So I have something to eat in order to not die of starvation.

As soon as you get to the bad thing that will happen if you don't do whatever it is, you have found your real problem. In this example, our real problem is that we want our plants to grow. To grow, they need water and sunlight. Sunlight happens without much worry. Water is more problematic. So that's our problem. How do we get water on our field?

Where people go wrong is that they lose sight of the real problem because they are instead focusing on a potential solution to the problem. They start thinking, I need it to rain, how do I do that? Do not turn a potential solution into a proxy problem. In other words, a problem that you think will solve your real problem, but that isn't your real problem.

Understanding not only what it is you ultimately are trying to accomplish, and what happens if you don't, is very motivating! In this case, I need my plants to grow or I will die.

Make sure you consider all of the different ways you might solve the problem. If you are focused on only one of your possible solutions, you are ignoring and not exploring your other possible options, which might be better. Consider all your options so you don't end up missing opportunities that are almost always easier and more effective.

Finally, proxy problems are often not solvable. You can't make it rain. Civilizations have literally collapsed trying to make it rain. Avoid making this mistake.

CHAPTER 6: ROOT CAUSES & REAL PROBLEMS

Let's assume you did your work and you asked yourself Why, and you are pretty sure that you're focusing on your real problem and not on a proxy problem that you think is important. Now you need to find out what is really causing your problem. To do this, you need to ask a lot of questions.

Why is this happening? How does it happen? Am I sure this information is correct?

To succeed, you need to be willing to ask questions, do some research, and evaluate the science behind it. Do not assume that you know why something is happening.

To help I'm going to introduce you to a critical thinking trick I like to call "The Rule of Threes." This is a mental shortcut that I use to help me make sure I am engaging in freethought and that I consider all of the possibilities. I was taught this by my boss at a tower company I used to work at. It turned out that everything we did could be broken down into three options. For instance, if you need access to land in order to put a tower on it, you could purchase the land, lease it, or get an easement onto it. You have at least three options. Most people think you can just purchase it or lease/rent land. There's actually a third option. The people who take the time to think of the third scenario are usually the ones that figure out how to creatively, effectively, and economically solve their problems.

Notice that I said my problem is that I need access to use land – not that I need land. Needing land is a proxy problem. Needing to access the land was the real problem we had. The difference is minor, but it's the difference between a successful strategy and a more costly strategy. Any money we didn't spend on acquiring access to land was money we could spend on something else.

The reason I want you to think of at least three options is because all humans, myself included, tend to think in terms of dichotomies. We can either eat-in or go out. You are either with us or against us. People who work in marketing use this tendency of ours, all the time, to trick us into thinking we need their product. Either you buy that cord-organizing piece of plastic or you can't possibly use anything else to wire up your television and sound system. They intentionally leave out alternatives.

The Rule of Three – Possible Causes

The first thing we need to do is think of at least three possible causes for our problem. Once you can think of three, you can think of four or five. The reason to do this is to make sure that you don't default to your assumptions about root causes. The problem is that once you have a bunch of possible causes, you have to figure out which ones are actually real and are actually impacting your real problem.

What I like to do is, once I've done my brainstorming, I narrow down my list to the three that I think are most likely. I then do my research and ask myself What do I know about this and what do I not know? What does the science say?

For example, let's talk about the subject of bullying. We know we want to stop bullying because it causes so much long-term harm to kids. What causes bullying? Do you know? Or do you just think you know? One of the reasons the bullying problem has been so difficult to solve is because people make a lot of assumptions about root causes. Is it bad parents? Mental illness? Sociopath? Enabled? Inherently evil?

One of the ways to tell that people are either working on a proxy problem or that they don't really know what is causing their problem, is that they fail to solve the problem.

In the case of bullying, science tells us that it is a learned behavior, meaning it's rewarded. Good parents can produce bullying children because parenting has very little to do with it. Shocking, I know. The point is, until we start focusing on the real root cause of our problem, we won't solve it!

Be skeptical about what you think the causes of your problems are. Think of at least three possible causes, or more, then use research and science to figure out which of your possible causes are real and which ones are just assumptions. Don't spend time on proxy problems or proxy causes.

CHAPTER 7: REAL SOLUTIONS TO REAL PROBLEMS

Let's assume that you are working on creating a solution to your real problem and that you understand what is really causing it. Now what? You now need a solution that will positively impact the root cause so that you can really solve your problem.

We are going to use the rule of three again. We are going to consider at least three possible solutions to our problem. We aren't going to go with the first person who comes along and offers us a solution. We are going to look for solutions that really do work to impact the real root cause of our problem. Once we have researched potential solutions, we are going to narrow our focus down to the three solutions that are most likely to work. Spend time properly defining your problem and the rest becomes much easier.

We know what our real problem is, so we will not get side-tracked on interesting, but pointless, proxy problems. We know what we need to do to solve our problem because we figured out what is really causing it. This helps us narrow down potential solutions to things that actually have a decent chance of working. We aren't looking for solutions that solve proxy problems and we also aren't looking for solutions to assumed causes. We are looking for real solutions to the real causes of our real problems.

I always like to narrow down my possibilities to three and then do a side-by-side comparison to choose the best one. Sticking to my rule of three, I have three criteria by which I judge potential solutions:

1. It's focused on solving the root cause of my real problem.

2. It has real science to back it up, meaning it actually works and isn't just a placebo solution.

3. Is it cost effective and easy to implement, given the real resources at my disposal.

This last bit is important because if it costs more than I can afford or it takes more resources than I have at my disposal, it won't work because I won't be able to implement it.

For Example:

I run an online business selling online courses. I have several problems running my company. I need to have a way for people to register for courses. I need to accept payment, otherwise I won't get paid. And I need to make sure people who sign up are registered into my online course system.

My first option is to do it manually. Have people write me or call me and send me a check, at which point I manually place them in the course. That would work, but it is time consuming and slow, and not an ideal solution.

My second option is I can automate things. I can use online forms to capture the information and online payment systems to allow people to pay online when they register. I can use scripts to automatically transfer that information into a format that I can use to upload the weekly registrations into my course system.

My third option is I can pay someone to do it for me. In fact, there's an online system that I can purchase that would do all of this for me and would integrate into my website quite well. That system costs in excess of $10k. Not exactly easy money to find when you are a startup. But it's certainly an option.

All three options solve my real problem and all three will work. The deciding factor is: Can I really implement it?

I chose option two, to set up automations to make it work. It's a little more time consuming than having someone else do it, but it's way more cost effective. The time it takes is about three hours per week. I now have a solution that really solves my problem, is cost effective, and makes good use of the real resources at my disposal. A reality based strategy that really works. Success!

CHAPTER 8: EXAMPLES

In this chapter I will provide examples of these techniques in order to give a little bit more perspective on how this really works when developing a strategy.

Effective Reality Based Strategies takes into account the following:

- **The Real problem** that really needs to be solved

- **The Real Root Causes** of that problem

- Real Solutions that have a **Real Impact** on the **Root Causes**

- **Really Achievable** – i.e., I have the resources required to create that impact

Example of a Proxy Problem

An example of a **Proxy Problem** is the climate change debate. While I was teaching a course in Socratic Jujutsu, otherwise known as how to win arguments without arguing, one of my students wanted to know how to convince people climate change is human-caused. I asked her why do you want to do that? I wondered why she cared whether people think it's caused by humans or not.

She thought she needed people to agree that climate change is caused by humans, in order to get them to adopt the policy changes she thinks are needed.

Getting people to agree that climate change is caused by humans is not her real problem. It is a proxy problem. It's one of many possible solutions to her real problem. Her real problem was the policy changes she wanted. There are a multitude of ways to get policies enacted. As long as she was focused on getting consensus on it being human-caused, she wasn't working on getting policy consensus at all. She was focused on a proxy problem and was not understanding why her efforts were not bearing legislative fruit.

Example of a Real Root Cause Problem

An example of a **Root Cause problem** is Bullying. What causes bullying? We know that we want bullying to stop and it's easy to articulate why. But what causes the bully to bully? Bad parents? Mental illness? General levels of evilness?

Those are all assumptions. Choose one without finding out if it's true and you will fail to stop bullying. If you haven't read my work on bullying, I'm about to blow your mind.

It doesn't matter why a bully is bullying. It's irrelevant to getting them to stop.

Wanting to know why they bully is a proxy problem. We think that if we know why they bully, we can get them to stop. So we focus on why. Yet we never get to the solution of getting them to stop.

I realize that the question of Why does a bully bully, has the word WHY in it. But we need to ask the question, "Why do we want to know why a bully bullies?" The answer is because we want them to stop!

Always ask yourself why you are focusing on something to get to your root problem.

Trying to solve the riddle – Why does a bully bully? – is a proxy problem. It's taking time, resources, and energy away from the real problem, which is, "What can we do to make them stop?"

Once we focus on the fact that we want them to stop, we can focus on how to get them to stop. Knowing why they bully is in service to that goal. I'm not going to get into the science here. People bully because they are rewarded for it. Now that you know that, you can come up with potential solutions and start working on your strategy to make a bully stop, which involves removing their reward. Now that we know that we are in a position to look for solutions that will help us stop rewarding bullies.

A realistic assessment of your problem and the root causes of your problem are the foundation upon which a realistic and effective strategy are built.

Example of a Real Solution that has a Realistic Impact Problem.

An example of a **Real Solution Problem** is Change Management.

There are several reasons why attempts to create change fail:

- The proposed solution doesn't work

- The proposed solution is a fix for a problem that doesn't exist. People change and it doesn't impact anything. The original problem is still there.

- The proposed solution does work but the people pushing for adoption don't know how to effectively create behavioral change so that the solution is actually adopted.

Do you know how to change a person's behavior using behavioral science? Have you ever thought to find out about how people change their behaviors, to find out how to do this successfully?

Summary

To create a strategy that will work

1) Focus on Real Problems – not Proxy Problems

2) Find the Real Root Cause of your problem using skepticism and science

3) Research to find out what really works to solve the problem.

4) Make sure your strategy is Really Doable using the resources at your disposal.

CHAPTER 9: ABOUT THE AUTHOR:

Jennifer Hancock is a mom, author of several books, and founder of Humanist Learning Systems. Jennifer is unique in that she was raised as a freethinker and is considered one of the top speakers and writers in the world of Humanism today. Her professional background is varied including stints in both the for profit and non-profit sectors. She has served as Director of Volunteer Services for the Los Angeles SPCA, sold international franchise licenses for a biotech firm, was the Manager of Acquisition Group Information for a ½ billion-dollar company and served as the executive director for the Humanists of Florida. When she became a mother, she decided to stay at home. But that didn't last long. Shortly after her son was born, she published her first book, The Humanist Approach to Happiness: Practical Wisdom. Her speaking and teaching business coalesced into the founding of Humanist Learning Systems which provides online personal and professional development training in humanistic business management and science based harassment training that actually works.

More Learning from Jennifer Hancock

OTHER BOOKS BY JENNIFER HANCOCK

- The Humanist Approach to Happiness
- Jen Hancock's Handy Humanism Handbook
- The Bully Vaccine
- The Humanist Approach to Grief and Grieving
- How to Win Arguments Without Arguing
- Why Bullies Bully & How to Stop Them Using Science

COURSES TAUGHT BY JENNIFER HANCOCK

- Workplace Bullying for HR professionals
- Living Made Simpler
- An Introduction to Humanism
- Socratic Jujitsu: How to Win Arguments Without Argument
- Why Conflict Resolution Doesn't Work When the Problem is Bullying

- Bridging the Generational Divide: Millennials vs. Boomers
- Ending Harassment and Retaliation in the Workplace
- Why is Change so Hard?
- Principles of Humanistic Management
- 7 Sins of Staff Management
- How to Handle Cranky Customer Problems
- New Manager Orientation
- Humanist Group Leadership Lessons
- Sexual harassment training that works – general
- Sexual harassment training that works – AB 1825
- Stop Bullying in our Workplace – Staff Training
- Sexual Harassment Compliance Training
- No Fear Act training
- Planning for Personal Success!
- Talking to your child about death

- [The Bully Vaccine Toolkit](#)
- [How to talk to your child's school about bullying](#)
- [Why Bullies Bully & How to Stop Them](#)

CONNECT WITH ME ONLINE:
- Twitter: http://twitter.com/#!/JentheHumanist
- Facebook: http://www.facebook.com/JentheHumanist
- Or sign up for my mailing list: http://eepurl.com/c3LuI

#####

www.ingramcontent.com/pod-product-compliance
Lightning Source LLC
Chambersburg PA
CBHW030103230526
45471CB00003B/1224